THE
MEMORY
JOGGER™
for Education

*A Pocket Guide
of Tools for
Continuous Improvement
in Schools*

© **GOAL/QPC** 1992
12B Manor Parkway, Salem, NH 03079-2862
800-643-4316
603-893-1944

Fax: 603-870-9122
E-mail: service@goalqpc.com
Web site: www.goalqpc.com

First Edition
10 9
Any reproduction of any part of this publication without the written permission of **GOAL/QPC** is prohibited.

ISBN 1-879364-24-7

GOAL/QPC
is a nonprofit research and training organization striving to help educational institutions continuously improve their **Q**uality, **P**roductivity, and **C**ompetitiveness.

Acknowledgements

The Memory Jogger™ for Education was adapted from *The Memory Jogger™*, compiled and edited by Michael Brassard of **GOAL/QPC**. Special thanks to Diane Ritter of **GOAL/QPC** for her counsel and contribution of statistical materials. This education edition was revised and assembled by Ann McManus with input and review by members of **GOAL/QPC**'s Education Team: Casey Collett, Marley Love-Goodnight, Diane Ritter, and Sue Tucker.

GOAL/QPC also gratefully acknowledges the special contribution of ideas, suggestions, and materials from the Marietta, GA school system, Collett & Associates, the J. DeMott Company, and the Superintendents' Focus Group of the Merrimack Valley, MA, Holden, MA, and Peterborough, NH.

GOAL/QPC welcomes your comments and/or submissions of new ideas for the tools in this edition of *The Memory Jogger™ for Education*.

Send to: *The Memory Jogger™ for Education*
GOAL/QPC
12B Manor Parkway
Salem, NH 03079-2862

Purpose

This handbook is designed to help public and private educators on elementary, secondary, and post-secondary levels to IMPROVE DAILY THE PROCEDURES, SYSTEMS, QUALITY, COST, AND OUTCOMES RELATED TO YOUR JOB. This continuous improvement process is the focus of today's QUALITY REVOLUTION.

In schools that are involved in this revolution, this continuous improvement process has two components:

1. Philosophy
2. Problem-Solving/Graphical Techniques

1. PHILOSOPHY
There are common points in the operating philosophies of these schools. They are as follows:
- Improving quality by removing the causes of problems in the system **inevitably** leads to improved productivity.
- The person doing the job is most knowledgeable about that job.
- People want to be involved and do their jobs well.
- Every person wants to feel like a valued contributor.
- More can be accomplished by working together to improve the system than having individual contributors working around the system.
- A structured problem-solving process using graphical techniques produces better solutions than an unstructured process.
- Graphical problem-solving techniques let you know where you are, where the variations lie, the relative importance of problems to be solved, and whether the changes made have had the desired impact.

- Adversarial relationships between labor and management are counterproductive and outmoded.
- Every organization has undiscovered "gems" waiting to be developed.

2. PROBLEM-SOLVING/GRAPHICAL TECHNIQUES
The rest of this handbook consists of practical descriptions, instructions, and examples of the following techniques:

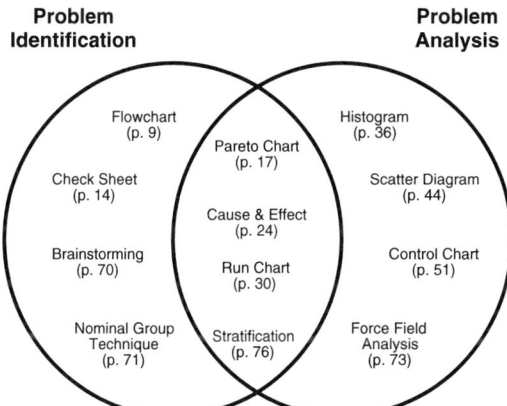

Notice that charts can be used for different purposes in various stages of the problem-solving process. For example, the tools included in the intersecting portion of this **VENN DIAGRAM** can be used in both the problem identification and problem analysis phase of problem-solving.

TECHNIQUE
Task

1. Decide which problem will be addressed first (or next).

2. Arrive at a statement that describes the problem in terms of what it is specifically, where it occurs, when it happens, and its extent.

3. Develop a complete picture of all the possible causes of the problem.

4. Agree on the basic cause(s) of the problem.

5. Develop an effective and implementable solution and action plan.

6. Implement the solution and establish needed monitoring procedures and charts.

SELECTION GUIDE
Techniques

- Flow Chart (p. 9)
- Check Sheet (p. 14)
- Pareto Chart (p. 17)

- Brainstorming (p. 70)
- Nominal Group Technique (p. 71)

- Check Sheet (p. 14)
- Pareto Chart (p. 17)
- Run Chart (p. 30)

- Histogram (p. 36)
- Pie Chart (p. 75)
- Stratification (p. 76)

- Check Sheet (p. 14)
- Cause & Effect Diagram (p. 24)
- Brainstorming (p. 70)

- Check Sheet (p. 14)
- Pareto Chart (p. 17)
- Scatter Diagram (p. 44)

- Brainstorming (p. 70)
- Nominal Group Technique (p. 71)

- Brainstorming (p. 70)
- Force Field Analysis (p. 73)
- Team Presentation (p. 74)

- Pie Chart (p. 75)
- Add'l Bar Graphs (p. 77)

- Pareto Chart (p. 17)
- Histogram (p. 36)

- Control Chart (p. 51)
- Stratification (p. 76)

HOW TO USE *THE MEMORY JOGGER*™

The Memory Jogger™ for Education is designed as a convenient and quick reference guide to be used on the job. It is therefore organized around symbols and color highlights that are eye-catching and easy to remember. The following is a legend explaining each symbol and its use.

Making Ready An important step in a problem-solving process is selecting the right tool for the situation. Each section on a new tool will begin with a boxed description that describes when it should be used. Always check this feature first to ensure that the tool meets your needs.

Cruising Turn to this portion of each section to find construction guidelines. This is the action phase that provides you with step-by-step instructions and helpful formulas. Turn to this feature in each section when you have basic how-to questions.

Finishing The Course  This portion of each section shows each tool in its final form. There are examples from Operations (Administration), Instruction (Faculty), and Classroom (Students) to display the widespread applications of each tool. Refer to this portion when you need to see the proper form of the finished charting technique.

Caution The boxed portion at the end of each section describes helpful construction and interpretation tips for that charting technique. Be sure to use this section to avoid making some of the most common mistakes when constructing and analyzing these tools.

Flowchart: When you need to identify the actual ideal paths that any process or service follows in order to identify deviations.

FLOWCHART

A Flowchart is a pictorial representation showing all of the steps of a process. Flowcharts provide excellent documentation of a program and can be a useful tool for examining how various steps in a process are related to each other. Flowcharting uses easily recognizable symbols to represent the type of processing performed.

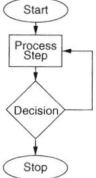

By studying these charts you can often uncover loopholes that are potential sources of trouble. Flowcharts can be applied to anything, from the travels of an invoice or the flow of materials, to the steps in making a curriculum decision or describing a learning process.

The Flowchart is most widely used in problem identification in a process called IMAGINEERING. The people with important knowledge about the process meet to:
1. Draw a Flowchart of what steps the process *actually* follows.
2. Draw a Flowchart of what steps the process *should* follow if everything worked right.
3. Compare the two charts to find where they are different because this is where the problems arise.

Flowchart—Operations Example
Attendance Monitoring

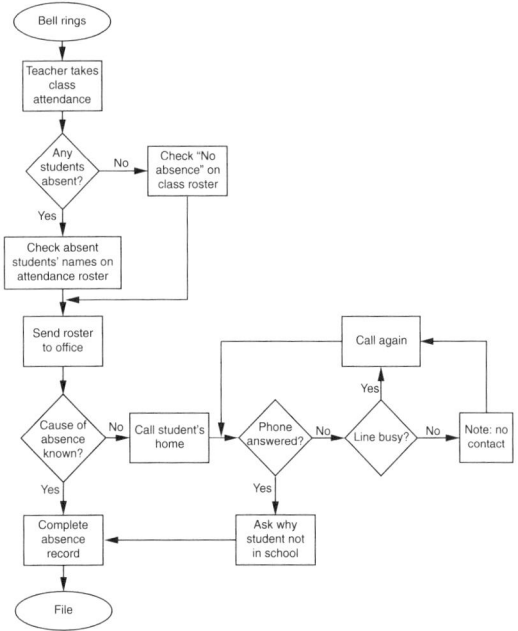

Flowchart—Instruction Example
Photocopy Process

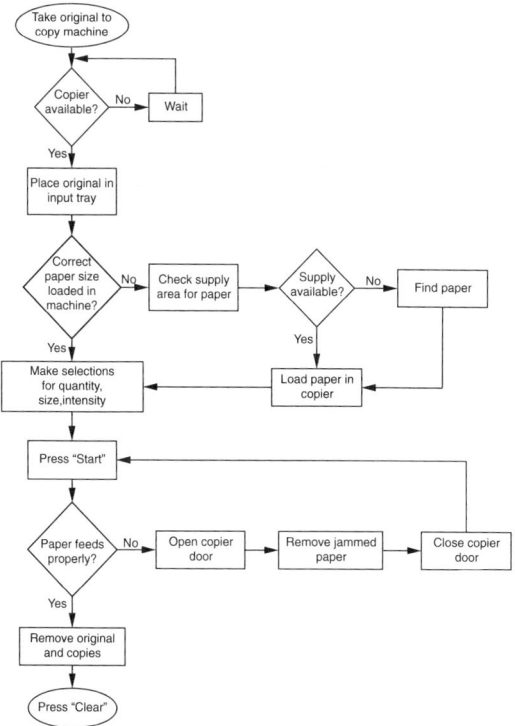

Flowchart—Classroom Example
Turning On A Hard Drive PC

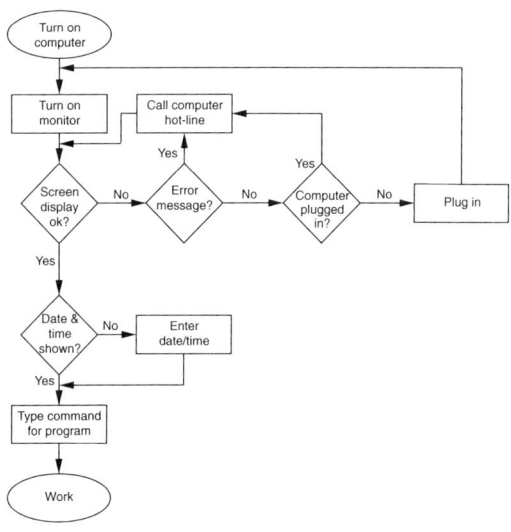

Construction/Interpretation Tips Flowchart

- Define the boundaries of the process clearly.
- Use the simplest symbols possible.
- Make sure every feedback loop has an escape.
- There is usually only one output arrow out of a *process* box. Otherwise, it may require a *decision* diamond.

Check Sheet: When you need to gather data that is based on sample observations to begin to detect patterns. This is the logical starting point in most problem-solving cycles.

CHECK SHEET

Check Sheets are simply easy-to-understand forms used to answer the question, "How often are certain events happening?" The Check Sheet starts the process of translating opinions into facts. Constructing a Check Sheet involves the following steps:

1. Agree on the event being observed. Everyone has to be looking for the same thing.
2. Decide on a time period to collect data. This could range from hours to weeks.
3. Design a form that is clear and easy to use, with columns clearly labeled and adequate space for entering data.
4. Collect the data consistently and honestly. Make sure there is time allowed for this data-gathering task.

Problem	Month			
	1	2	3	Total
A	II	II	I	5
B	I	I	I	3
C	IIII	II	IIII	12
Total	8	5	7	20

Check Sheet—Operations Example
Attendance Monitoring

Reasons	Month					
	Day 1	Day 2	Day 3	Day 4	Day 5	Total
Illness	||||	|||| |||	||||	|||	||||	26
Family Issues	|||| ||	||||	|||| |||	||||	||||	29
Transportation	|||	||||	||	||	||	13
Truancy	|||	||		||	|||| |||	15
Other	||||	||	||			||||		15
Total	22	20	17	13	26	98

Check Sheet—Instruction Example
Interruptions in Classroom/Week

Reasons	Day					
	1	2	3	4	5	Total
PA Announcement	||||	||	||||	||	||||	17
Deliver Forms	||			||			||	8
Student Called Out				||	|||			7
Special Classes	||||	||||	||||	||	||||		21
Telephone	||	|||	||					9
Visitors					||		3
Total	13	12	15	11	14	65

Check Sheet—Classroom Example
Keyboard Errors in Class Assignment

Mistakes	March			
	1	2	3	Total
Centering	II	III	III	8
Spelling	JHT II	JHT JHT I	JHT	23
Punctuation	JHT JHT JHT	JHT JHT	JHT JHT JHT	40
Missed Paragraph	II	I	I	4
Wrong Numbers	III	IIII	III	10
Wrong Page #'s	I	I	II	4
Tables	IIII	JHT	IIII	13
Total	34	35	33	102

Construction/Interpretation Tips
Check Sheet

- Make sure that observations/samples are as representative as possible.
- Make sure the sampling process is efficient so that people have time to do it.
- In doing a Check Sheet, you may not be aware that the population (universe) being sampled is non-homogeneous (not from the same teacher, class, etc.). The population must be homogeneous. If not, it must first be stratified (grouped), with each grouping sampled individually.

Pareto Chart: When you need to display the relative importance of all the problems or conditions in order to: choose the starting point for problem solving, monitor success, or identify the basic cause of a problem.

PARETO CHART

A Pareto Chart is a special form of vertical bar graph that helps you determine which problems to solve in what order. Doing a Pareto Chart based upon either Check Sheets or other forms of data collection helps direct attention and efforts to the truly important problems. You will generally gain more by working on the tallest bar than tackling the smaller bars.

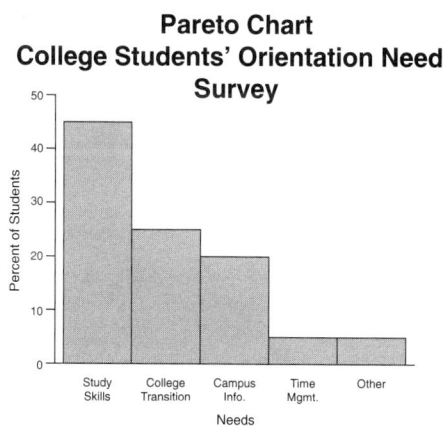

Steps in Constructing a Pareto Chart

1. Select the problems that are to be compared and rank-ordered by:

   a. **Brainstorming,** e.g., "What are our major quality problems in School A or Department A?"

   b. **Using Existing Data,** e.g., "Let's take a look at School A's quality reports over the last month to find the major problem areas."

2. Select a common unit of measurement, such as annual cost or frequency.

3. Select the time period to be studied, such as 8 hours, 5 days, or 4 weeks.

4. Gather the necessary data for each category, e.g., "Problem A occurred X times in the last 6 months" or "Problem B cost X dollars in the last 2 months."

5. Compare the frequency or cost of each category relative to all other categories, e.g., "Problem A happened 75 times; Problem B happened 107 times; Problem C happened 35 times," or "Problem A cost $750 annually; Problem B cost $535 annually."

6. List the categories from left to right on the horizontal axis of the Pareto Chart in order of decreasing frequency or cost. The categories containing the fewest items can be combined into an "other" category, which is placed on the extreme right as the last bar.

7. Above each classification or category, draw a rectangle whose height represents the frequency or cost in that classification.

Additional Features of Pareto Charts:

- Often the "raw data" is recorded on the left vertical axis with a percentage scale on the right vertical axis. Make sure that the two axes are drawn to scale, so that the 100% mark is opposite the total frequency or cost, and the 50% mark is opposite the halfway point in the raw data.

- From the top of the tallest bar and moving upward from left to right, a line can be added that shows the cumulative frequency of the categories. This answers such questions as, "How much of the total is accounted for by the first three categories?"

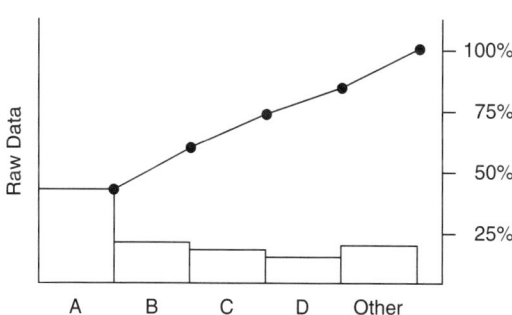

DIFFERENT USES OF A PARETO CHART

1. To identify the most important problems through the use of different measurement criteria, such as frequency or cost.
   Lesson: The most frequent problems are not always the most costly.

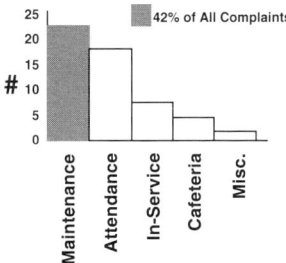

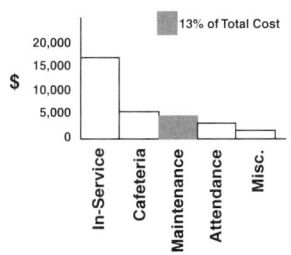

2. To analyze data in different groupings, e.g., by instruction, by day, by events.
   Lesson: If clear differences don't emerge, regroup the data. Use your imagination.

Pareto Analysis of Classroom Interruptions

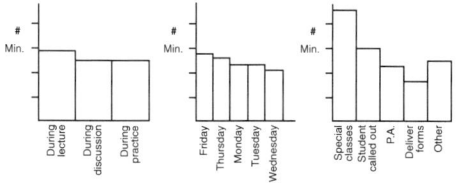

Note: After the data is graphed in three different ways, it is clear that "special classes" is the major cause of interruptions.

3. To measure the impact of changes made in a process, such as before and after comparisons.
   Lesson: You don't know how much better you are if you don't know where you were before the change.

Homework Process

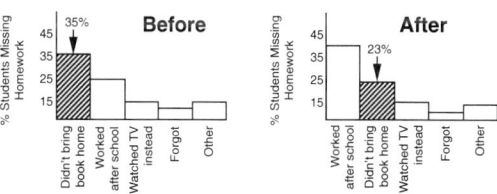

Note: Change the process by assigning homework that does not need a text, by providing reminders at the end of the school day to bring home essential texts for homework, or by providing time for students to do homework in school.

4. To break down broad causes into more and more specific parts.
   Lesson: Cure the cause, not the symptom.

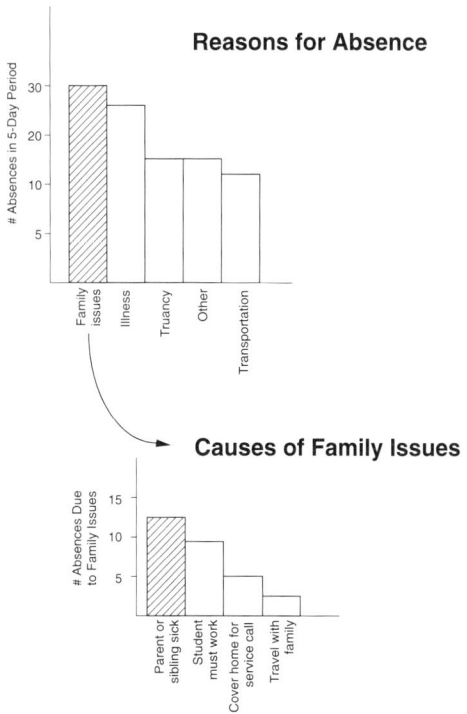

Construction/Interpretation Tips Pareto Chart

- Use common sense. Two key customer complaints may deserve more attention than 100 other complaints, depending on who the customer is and what the complaint is.
- Mark the chart clearly to show the standard of measurement ($, %, or #).

Cause & Effect Diagram: When you need to identify, explore, and display the possible causes of a specific problem or condition.

CAUSE & EFFECT DIAGRAM

The Cause & Effect Diagram represents the relationship between some "effect" and all the possible "causes." The effect or problem is stated on the right side of the chart and the major influences or causes are listed on the left.

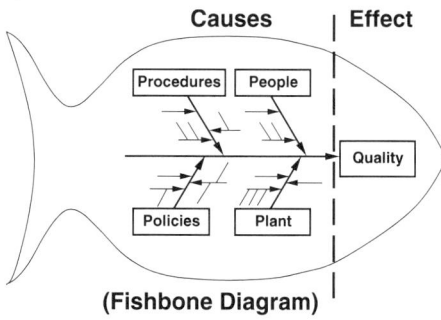

(Fishbone Diagram)

Cause & Effect Diagrams are drawn to clearly illustrate the various causes affecting a process by sorting out and relating the causes. For every effect there are likely to be several major categories of causes. The major causes might be summarized under four categories referred to as the 4P's: Policies, Procedures, People, and Plant. It may be helpful in some circumstances to consider the 4M's: Manpower, Machines, Methods, and Materials. Remember that these categories are only suggestions. You may use any major category that emerges or helps people think creatively.

A well-detailed Cause & Effect Diagram will take on the shape of fishbones and hence the alternate name, Fishbone Diagram. From this well-defined list of possible causes, the most likely are identified and selected for further analysis. When examining each cause, look for things that have changed, deviations from the norm or patterns. Remember, try to cure the cause and not the symptoms of the problem. Push the causes back as much as is practically possible by asking "Why?" for each "bone."

STEPS IN CONSTRUCTING A CAUSE & EFFECT DIAGRAM

1. Generate the causes needed to build a Cause & Effect Diagram in one of two ways:
    a. Brainstorm possible causes without previous preparation.
    b. Ask members of the team to spend time between meetings tracking possible causes using Check Sheets and to examine the process steps closely.
2. Construct the actual Cause & Effect Diagram by:
    a. Placing the problem statement in a box on the right.
    b. Drawing the traditional major cause category steps in the process, or any causes that are helpful in organizing the most important factors.
    c. Placing the Brainstormed ideas in the appropriate major categories.
    d. For each cause ask, "Why does it happen?" and list responses as branches off the major causes.
3. To find the most basic causes of the problem:
    a. Look for causes that appear repeatedly.
    b. Reach a team consensus.
    c. Gather data to determine the relative frequencies of the different causes.

Cause & Effect Diagram— Operations Example

Building a School's Community Image

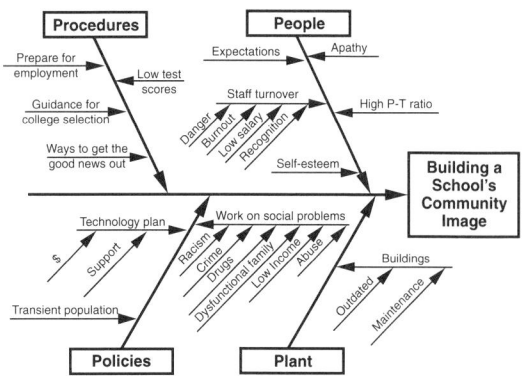

Cause & Effect Diagram—
Instruction Example

Why Students Drop Out of School

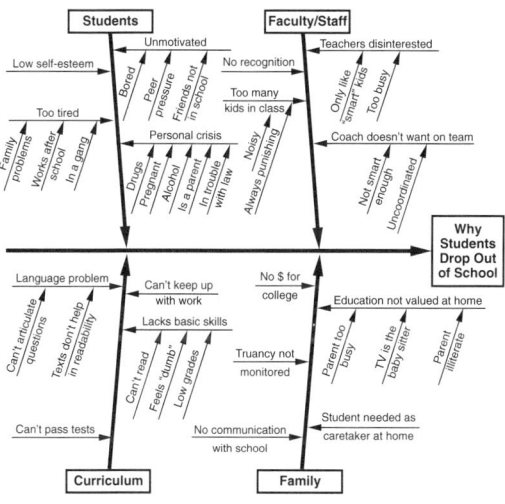

Cause & Effect Diagram—
Classroom Example

College, secondary, and vocational-technical school students will relate to a learning issue that affects their daily lives.

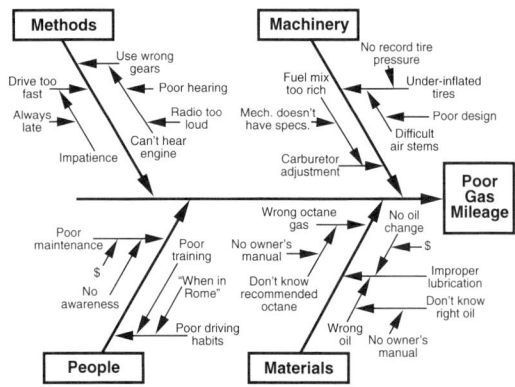

Construction/Interpretation Tips
Cause & Effect Diagram

- Try not to go far beyond the area of control of the group in order to minimize frustration.
- If ideas are slow in coming use the major cause categories as catalysts, e.g., "What in *policies* is causing . . .?"
- Use as few words as possible.
- Make sure everyone agrees completely on the problem statement.
- The most widely used type of Cause & Effect Diagram is the **Dispersion Analysis** which is shown in *The Memory Jogger*™. It is constructed by placing individual causes within each "major" cause category and asking of each item, "Why does this cause (dispersion) happen?" Other common types of Cause & Effect Diagrams are the following:
  a. **Process Classification Cause & Effect Diagrams** sequentially list all the steps in a process. The same cause category arrows as in Dispersion Analysis branch off the line between each process step. The same question then applied to each cause category as in the Dispersion Analysis type diagram.
  b. **Cause Enumeration Cause & Effect Diagrams** are almost identical to the Dispersion Analysis type. The only real difference is that Cause Enumeration first organizes all the possible causes in list form and then places them in the major cause categories.

> **Run Chart:** When you need to do the simplest possible display of trends within observation points over a specified time period.

RUN CHART

Run Charts are used to monitor a process to see whether or not the long-range average is changing.

Run Charts are the simplest tools to construct and use. Points are plotted on the graph in the order in which they become available. It is common to graph the results of a process such as enrollment, schedules, typographical errors, or productivity as they vary over time.

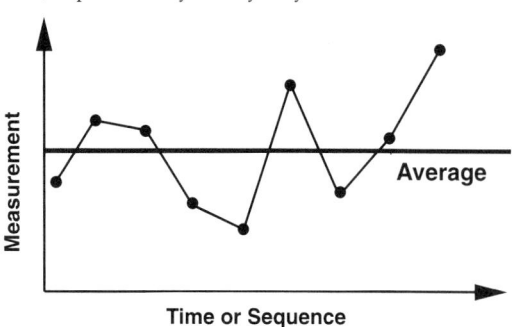

A danger in using a Run Chart is the tendency to see every variation in data as being important. The Run Chart, like the other charting techniques, should be **used to focus attention on truly vital changes in the process.**

One of the most valuable uses of Run Charts is to identify meaningful trends or shifts in the average. For example, when monitoring any process, we should expect to find an equal number of points falling above and below the average. However, when **nine** points "run" on one side of the average it indicates a statistically unusual event and that the average has changed. Such changes should always be investigated. If the shift is favorable, the shift should be made a permanent part of the system. If the shift is unfavorable, the cause should be eliminated.

An alternate type of pattern that can occur is a trend of six or more points steadily increasing or decreasing with no reversals. Neither pattern would be expected to happen based on random chance. Thus, this would likely indicate an important change and the need to investigate.

Run Chart—Operations Example
Class Size Trends Over a Ten-Year Period

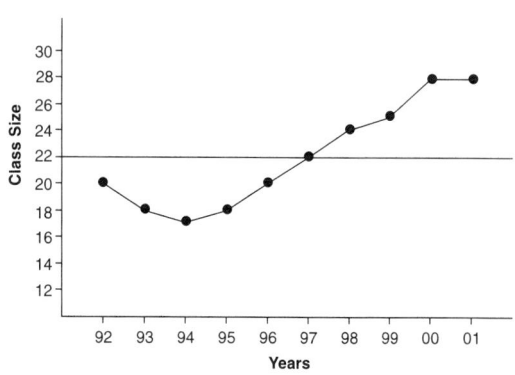

Run Chart—Instruction Example
Percent of Students Passing Grade-Level Reading Test

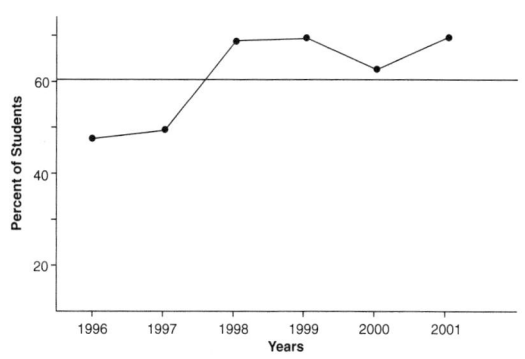

Run Chart—Classroom Example
Time Spent on Homework/Day

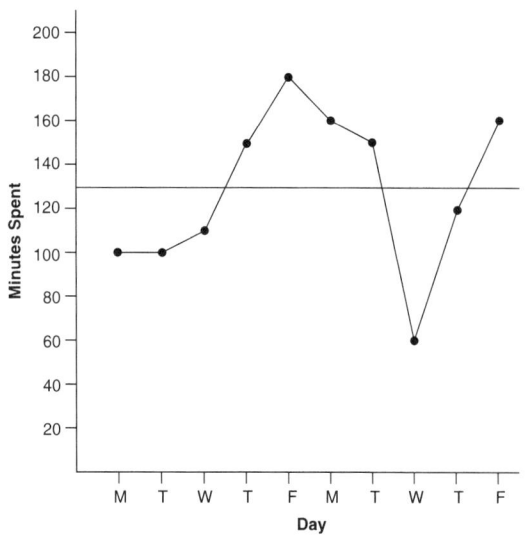

Construction/Interpretation Tips
Run Chart

- The *y-axis* is the vertical side of the graph.
- The *x-axis* is the horizontal side of the graph.
- A marked point indicates the measurement or quantity observed or sampled at one point in time.
- Data points should be connected for easy use and interpretation.
- The time period covered and unit of measurement used must be clearly marked.
- Collected data must be kept in the order that it was gathered. Since it is tracking a characteristic over time, the sequence of data points is critical.

Histogram: When you need to discover and display the distribution of data by bar graphing the number of units in each category.

HISTOGRAM

As we have already seen with the Pareto Chart, it is helpful to display in bar graph form the frequency with which certain events occur (frequency distribution). The Pareto Chart, however, only deals with characteristics of a product or service, such as incidence or a particular problem. A Histogram displays the distribution of measurement data, such as scores, size, or temperature. This is critical since we know that all repeated events will produce results that vary over time. A Histogram reveals the amount of variation that any process has within it. A typical Histogram would look like this:

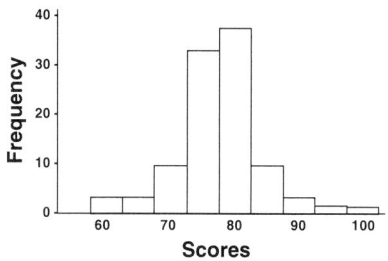

The Histogram pictured here shows the greatest number of units at the center measurement with roughly an equal number of units falling on either side of that point. Many repeated samples of data under statistical control follow this pattern. Other data displays patterns with the data "piled up" at points away from the center. Such a distribution is called "skewed." The important thing to remember is that you are looking for surprises such as distributions that should be naturally "normal" but are not. The same is true for predictably skewed distributions. In addition to the shape of the distribution you are also looking for:

a. Whether the "spread" of the curve falls within specifications. If not, how much falls outside of specifications. (VARIABILITY)
b. Whether the curve is centered at the right place. Are most items on the "high or low side"? (SKEWNESS)

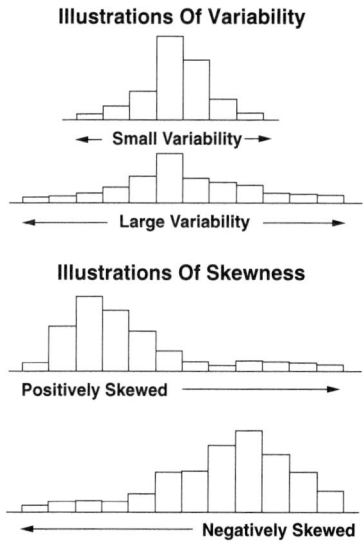

STEPS IN CONSTRUCTING A HISTOGRAM

There will be more detailed instructions for constructing Histograms than for most of the other tools. This is being stressed because of the confusion that seems to be created when deciding on the number of classes (bars) and the class boundaries.

Start with an unorganized set of at least 50 numbers such as the following:

7:57	7:57	8:08	8:07	8:08	8:06
8:00	8:04	8:00	8:05	8:02	7:54
8:02	8:03	8:02	8:04	8:04	8:02
8:03	7:57	7:56	8:08	7:58	7:54
8:00	8:01	7:58	8:08	8:00	7:53
8:10	8:06	8:06	8:00	8:02	7:58
8:07	8:05	7:56	8:00	8:01	8:00
7:59	8:00	7:58	8:04	8:06	8:01
8:05	8:00	7:59	8:06	7:59	8:00
7:58	8:04	8:02	8:02	8:10	8:00

These numbers refer to the morning arrival time of a school bus at a school.

1. **Count the number of data points in the data set.** In our example above there are 60 data points (n=60).

2. **Determine the range, R, for the entire data set.** The range is the smallest value in the set of data subtracted from the largest value. In our case, the range is equal to 8:10 minus 7:53. Thus, the range equals 17 minutes.

3. **Divide the range value into a certain number of classes, referred to as K.** The table below provides an approximate guideline for dividing your set of data into a reasonable number of classes. For our example, 60 data points would be broken down into 6-10 classes. We will use K=10 classes, for ease of computation.

Number Of Data Points	Number Of Classes (K)
Under 50	5-7
50-100	6-10
100-250	7-12
Over 250	10-20

4. **Determine the class width, H.** A convenient formula is as follows:

$$H = \frac{R}{K} = \frac{17}{10} = 1.7$$

In most cases, it helps to round off H but carry the number to one more decimal point than in the original data set. For our purposes, 2.0 would appear appropriate, indicating that the class width for our example is 2 minutes, or :02.

---

[1] In previous printings this was referred to as "range value." It has been revised for greater clarity.

5. **Determine the class boundary, or end points.** To determine the class boundaries, find the smallest individual measurement in the data set. Use this number or round to the next appropriate lower number. This will be the lower end point for our first class boundary. In our example this would be 7:52. Now take this number and add the class width to it, 7:52 + :02 = 7:54. Thus, the next lower class boundary would begin at 7:54. The first class would be 7:52 and everything up to, but not including 7:54, 7:52 through 7:53:59. The second class would begin at 7:54 and be everything up to, **but not including** 7:56. This makes each class mutually exclusive, that is each of our data set points will fit into **one, and only one**, class. Finally, consecutively add the class width, :02, to the lowest class boundary until the correct number of classes, approximately 10, and containing the range of all our numbers, is obtained.

6. **Construct a frequency table based on the values computed above (number of classes, class width, class boundary).** The frequency table is actually a Histogram in a tabular form. A frequency table based on the arrival time data is shown below:

Class #	Class Boundaries	Mid-point	Frequency	Total
1	7:52-7:53:59	7:53	l	1
2	7:54-7:55:59	7:55	ll	2
3	7:56-7:57:59	7:57	ℍ	5
4	7:58-7:59:59	7:59	ℍ lll	8
5	8:00-8:01:59	8:01	ℍ ℍ llll	14
6	8:02-8:03:59	8:03	ℍ llll	9
7	8:04-8:05:59	8:05	ℍ lll	8
8	8:06-8:07:59	8:07	ℍ ll	7
9	8:08-8:09:59	8:09	ℍ	4
10	8:10-8:11:59	8:11	ll	2

7. **Construct the Histogram based on the frequency table.** A Histogram is a graphical picture of a frequency table. It provides us with a quick picture of the distribution for the measured characteristic. A Histogram for our example is shown below:

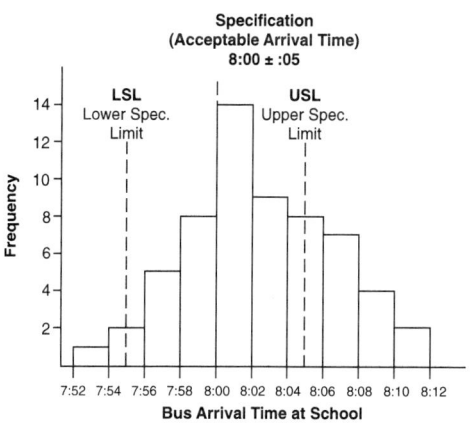

As pointed out earlier, the Histogram is an important diagnostic tool because it gives a "bird's-eye view" of the variation in a data set. In our case, the data appears to have a central tendency around 8:01. It also appears that the data creates close to a normal curve, indicating that the specification for the bus arrival time is 7:55 to 8:05, with a target of 8:00. Our Histogram shows that the process is running high and that attention needs to be paid to the causes of the later arrival times of this particular route's bus.

Histogram—Operations Example
Average Response Time to Maintenance Requests

Histogram—Instruction Example
% Scores on 20-Item Test

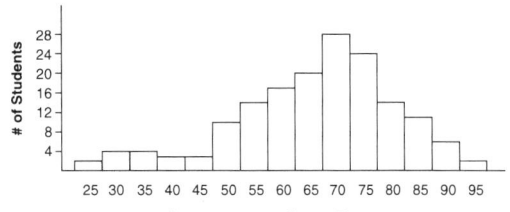

162 students were given a "true-false" test.

Histogram—Classroom Example
Students' Self-Rating of Mathematics Ability

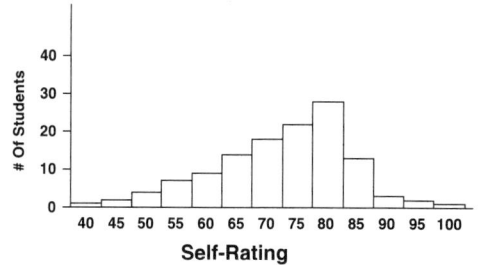

 Construction/Interpretation Tips Histogram

- The number of classes (bars in the graph) determines how much of a pattern will be visible.
- Some processes are naturally skewed; don't expect every distribution to follow a bell-shaped curve.
- Get suspicious of the accuracy of the data if the classes suddenly stop at one point (such as a specification limit) without some previous decline in number.
- Always look for *twin peaks* indicating that the data is coming from two or more different sources.

Scatter Diagram: When you need to display what happens to one variable when another variable changes in order to test a theory that the two variables are related.

SCATTER DIAGRAM

A Scatter Diagram is used to study the possible relationship between one variable and another. It shows possible **cause** and **effect** relationships. It cannot prove that one variable **causes** the other, but it does make it clear whether a relationship exists and the strength of that relationship.

A Scatter Diagram has a horizontal axis (x-axis), to represent the measurement values of one variable, and a vertical axis (y-axis), to represent the measurements of a second variable. A typical Scatter Diagram may look like this:

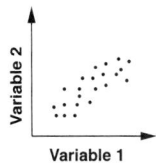

Notice how the plotted points form a clustered pattern. The direction and "tightness" of the cluster give a clue as to the strength of the relationship between variable 1 and variable 2. The more that this cluster resembles a straight line, the stronger the correlation between the variables. This makes sense since a straight line would mean that every time one variable would change the other changed by the same amount.

STEPS IN CONSTRUCTING A SCATTER DIAGRAM

1. **Collect 50 to 100 paired samples of data that you think may be related and construct a data sheet as follows:**

Person	Height	Weight
1	70 inches	160 lbs.
2	61 inches	180 lbs.
3	75 inches	220 lbs.
.	.	.
.	.	.
50	61 inches	105 lbs.

2. **Draw the horizontal and vertical axes of the diagram.** The values should get higher as you move up and to the right on each axis. The variable that's being investigated as the possible "cause" is usually on the horizontal and the "effect" variable is usually on the vertical.

3. **Plot the data on the diagram.** If you find the values being repeated, circle that point as many times as appropriate. The resulting diagram may look like this:

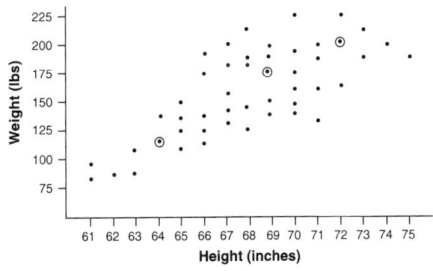

The following are the various patterns and meanings that Scatter Diagrams can have:

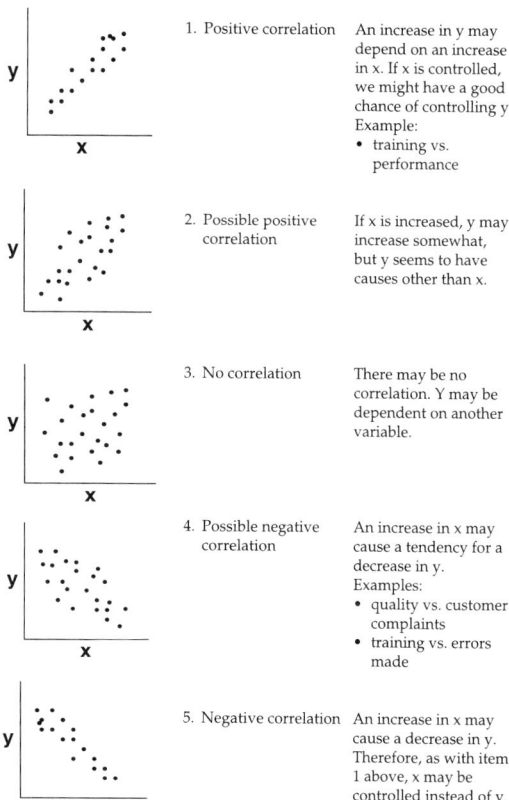

1. Positive correlation — An increase in y may depend on an increase in x. If x is controlled, we might have a good chance of controlling y. Example:
   - training vs. performance

2. Possible positive correlation — If x is increased, y may increase somewhat, but y seems to have causes other than x.

3. No correlation — There may be no correlation. Y may be dependent on another variable.

4. Possible negative correlation — An increase in x may cause a tendency for a decrease in y. Examples:
   - quality vs. customer complaints
   - training vs. errors made

5. Negative correlation — An increase in x may cause a decrease in y. Therefore, as with item 1 above, x may be controlled instead of y.

Scatter Diagram—Operations Example
Overtime/# of Billing Errors

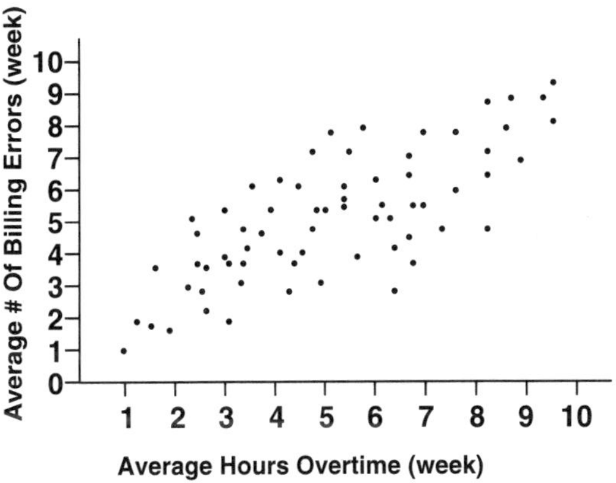
Average # Of Billing Errors (week)
0
1
2
3
4
5
6
7
8
9
10
1
2
3
4
5
6
7
8
9
10
Average Hours Overtime (week)

Scatter Diagram—Instruction Example
Students' Study Time/Test Scores

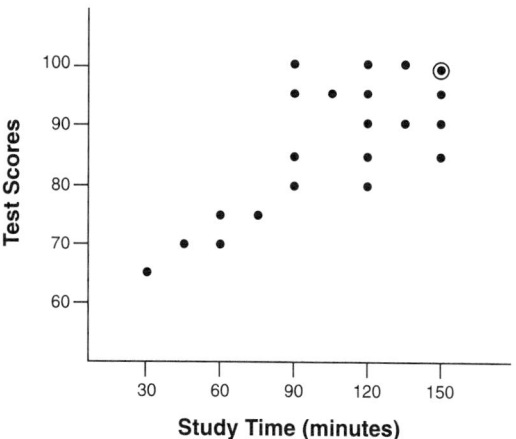

Scatter Diagram—Classroom Example
Students' After-School Jobs/Grades

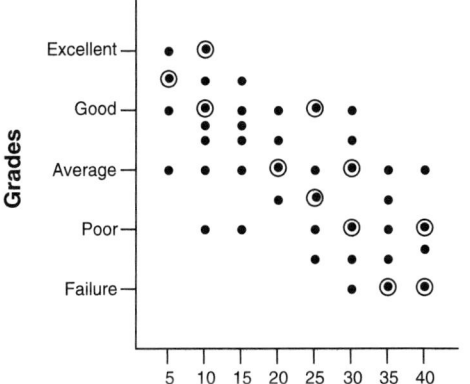

Construction/Interpretation Tips
Scatter Diagram

- A negative relationship (as y increases, x decreases) is as important as a positive relationship (as x increases, y increases).
- You can only say that x and y are related and not that one *causes* the other.
- The examples in this section were based on straight line correlations: y=ax+b. However, this is not the only form of relationship that can be routinely encountered: $y=e^x$, $y=x^2$, and $y^2=x$ are just a few of the many types that can occur.
- There are statistical tests available to test the exact degree of correlation but they are beyond the scope of this book.

Control Chart: When you need to discover how much variability in a process is due to random variation and how much is due to unique events/individual actions to determine whether a process is in statistical control.

CONTROL CHART

A Control Chart is simply a Run Chart with **statistically determined** upper (Upper Control Limit) and possibly lower (Lower Control Limit) lines drawn on either side of the process average.

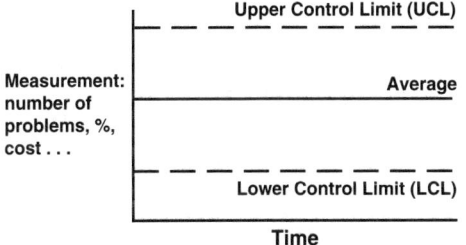

These limits are calculated by running a process untouched (i.e., according to standard procedures but without any extra "tweaking" adjustments), taking samples, and plugging the sample averages into the appropriate formula. You can now plot the sample averages onto a chart to determine whether any of the points fall between or outside of the limits or form unlikely patterns. If any of these happen, the process is said to be "out of control."

The fluctuation of the points within the limits results from variation built into the process. This ensues from **common causes** within the **system**, such as design, choice of course, rework, or suppliers and can only be affected by changing that system. However, points outside of the limits come from a **special cause** (such as human error, an unplanned event, or freak occurrences) that is not the way that the process normally operates, or from an unlikely combination of process steps. These special causes must be examined and addressed before the Control Chart can continue to be used as a monitoring tool. Once this is done, the process would be "in control" and samples can be taken at regular intervals to make sure that the process doesn't fundamentally change.

REMEMBER: "Control" doesn't necessarily mean that the product or service will meet your needs. It only means that the process is **consistent** (it may be consistently bad). For example:

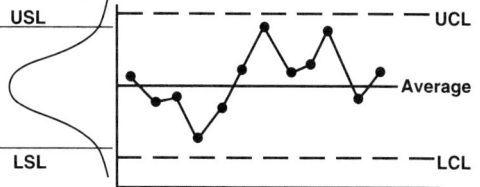

In this case, the process is in control but it is not capable of meeting the specification. The curve to the left of the Control Chart shows that the specification limits are narrower than the Control Charted process. Either you improve the process or you change the specifications. Just remember that specifications are what you think you need and control limits are what the process can do consistently.

STEPS IN CONSTRUCTING VARIABLES CONTROL CHARTS AND CRITICAL FORMULAS

Variables Control Chart:
Use when samples are expressed in **quantitative** units of measurement, such as length, weight, time, or scores.

$\bar{X}$—R Chart =

Plotting the Average & Range of Data Collected

1. Calculate the Average ($\bar{X}$) and Range (R) of each subgroup:

    $$\bar{X} = \frac{X_1 + X_2 + \ldots + X_n}{n}$$ n = # of samples

    $$R = X_{max} - X_{min}$$

2. Calculate the Process Average ($\bar{\bar{X}}$)

    $$\bar{\bar{X}} = \frac{\bar{X}_1 + \bar{X}_2 + \ldots + \bar{X}_k}{k}$$ k = # of subgroups (20-25 groups)

    and the Average Range ($\bar{R}$):

    $$\bar{R} = \frac{R_1 + R_2 + \ldots + R_k}{k}$$

3. Calculate the Control Limits:

    $UCL_{\bar{X}} = \bar{\bar{X}} + A_2\bar{R}$ $LCL_{\bar{X}} = \bar{\bar{X}} - A_2\bar{R}$

    $UCL_R = D_4\bar{R}$ $LCL_R = D_3\bar{R}$

Table of Factors for $\bar{X}$ & R Charts

Number of observations in subgroup (n)	Factors for $\bar{X}$ Chart	Factors for R Chart	
	A_2	Lower D_3	Upper D_4
2	1.880	0	3.268
3	1.023	0	2.574
4	0.729	0	2.282
5	0.577	0	2.114
6	0.483	0	2.004
7	0.419	0.076	1.924
8	0.373	0.136	1.864
9	0.337	0.184	1.816
10	0.308	0.223	1.777

CONSTRUCTION OF ATTRIBUTES CONTROL CHARTS AND CRITICAL FORMULAS

Attributes Control Chart:
Use when samples reflect **qualitative** characteristics, such as has/does not have, go/no go.

The p Chart = Proportion faulty

$$p = \frac{\text{number of flaws in subgroups}}{\text{number examined in subgroup}}$$

$$\bar{p} = \frac{\text{total number of flaws}}{\text{total number examined}}$$

$$UCL_p^* = \bar{p} + \frac{3\sqrt{\bar{p}(1-\bar{p})}}{\sqrt{n}} \qquad LCL_p^* = \bar{p} - \frac{3\sqrt{\bar{p}(1-\bar{p})}}{\sqrt{n}}$$

The np Chart = Number faulty

$$UCL_{np} = n\bar{p} + 3\sqrt{n\bar{p}(1-\bar{p})} \qquad LCL_{np} = n\bar{p} - 3\sqrt{n\bar{p}(1-\bar{p})}$$

The c Chart = Number of nonconformities with a constant sample size

$$\bar{c} = \frac{\text{total nonconformities}}{\text{number of subgroups}}$$

$$UCL_c = \bar{c} + 3\sqrt{\bar{c}} \qquad LCL_c = \bar{c} - 3\sqrt{\bar{c}}$$

The u Chart = Number of nonconformities with a varying sample size

$$\bar{u} = \frac{\text{total nonconformities}}{\text{total units examined}}$$

$$UCL_u^* = \bar{u} + \frac{3\sqrt{\bar{u}}}{\sqrt{n}} \qquad LCL_u^* = \bar{u} - \frac{3\sqrt{\bar{u}}}{\sqrt{n}}$$

* This formula creates changing control limits. To avoid this, use average sample sizes $\sqrt{\bar{n}}$ for samples that are ±20% of the average sample size. Calculate individual limits for the samples exceeding ±20%.

INTERPRETING CONTROL CHARTS

The process is said to be "out of control" if:

1. One or more points fall outside of the control limits
or:
2. When you divide the control chart into zones as follows:

```
_ _ _ _ _ _ _ _   Upper Control Limit
     Zone A       (UCL)
_____
     Zone B
_____
     Zone C
═════════════════ Centerline/Average
     Zone C
_____
     Zone B
_____
_ _ _Zone A_ _ _  Lower Control Limit
                  (LCL)
```

You should take note and examine what has changed and **possibly** make a process adjustment if:
a. Two out of three successive points are on the same side of the centerline in Zone A or beyond.
b. Four out of five successive points are on the same side of the centerline in Zone B or beyond.
c. Nine successive points are on one side of the centerline.
d. There are six or more consecutive increasing or decreasing points.
e. There are 14 points in a row, alternating up and down.
f. There are 15 points in a row within Zone C (above and below the centerline).

(see diagram page 56)

Tests for Control

COMMON QUESTIONS TO ASK WHEN INVESTIGATING AN OUT-OF-CONTROL PROCESS*

☐ Yes ☐ No   Are there differences in the measurement accuracy of the instruments used?

☐ Yes ☐ No   Are there differences in the methods used by different persons?

☐ Yes ☐ No   Is the process affected by the environment (e.g., temperature, humidity)?

☐ Yes ☐ No   Has there been a significant change in the environment?

☐ Yes ☐ No   Is the process affected by equipment wear?

☐ Yes ☐ No   Were any untrained people involved in the process at the time?

* **"Out of Control"** as defined by conditions on page 55.

COMMON QUESTIONS TO ASK WHEN INVESTIGATING AN OUT-OF-CONTROL PROCESS*

(Continued)

☐ Yes ☐ No Has there been a change in the source for raw materials (textbooks, supplies, equipment)?

☐ Yes ☐ No Is the process affected by personal fatigue?

☐ Yes ☐ No Has there been a change in maintenance procedures?

☐ Yes ☐ No Is the process/procedure being adjusted frequently?

☐ Yes ☐ No Did the samples come from different departments? faculty? equipment?

☐ Yes ☐ No Is anyone afraid to report "bad news"?

* **"Out of Control"** as defined by conditions on page 55.

Control Chart—Operations
Example X̄ & R Chart
Building Temperature Control

DATE										
TIME		8:00	8:30	9:00	9:30	10:00	10:30	11:00	11:30	12:00	12:30
SAMPLE MEASUREMENTS	1	-2	+1	+3	+2	-4	0	-1	-3	-6	+2
	2	-2	0	+1	+3	-3	0	+1	+2	+2	-1
	3	0	-1	-3	+5	0	-1	+2	-2	0	0
	4	0	-1	+1	+2	+1	+1	-1	+1	+4	+1
	5	-2	+1	0	+2	+3	-4	+3	+1	+4	+1
SUM		-6	0	+2	+14	-3	-4	+4	-1	+4	+3
AVERAGE, X̄		-1.2	0	+.4	+2.8	-.6	-.8	+.8	-.2	+.8	+.6
RANGE, R		2	2	6	3	7	5	4	5	10	3
NOTES											

Control Chart—Instruction Example
np Chart
Discipline Problems Requiring Intervention/Day

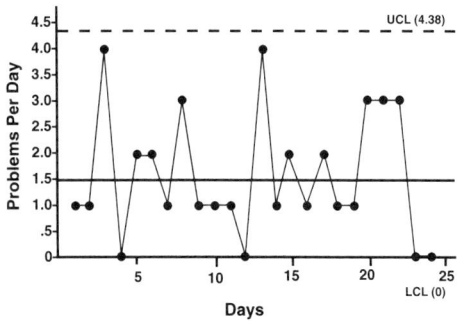

Control Chart—Classroom Example
Student Self-Monitoring of Daily Quiz Work

STEP 1

				Week					
1	2	3	4	5	6	7	8	9	10
55	90	100	70	55	75	100	65	70	100
75	95	75	100	65	85	95	65	85	80
65	60	75	65	95	65	65	90	60	65
80	60	65	60	70	65	85	90	65	60
80	55	65	60	70	65	70	60	75	80
$\bar{X}$=71	72	76	71	71	71	83	74	71	77
R=25	40	35	40	40	20	35	30	25	40

STEP 2

$$\bar{\bar{X}} = 73.7$$
$$\bar{R} = 33$$
$$n = 5$$
$$k = 10$$

STEP 3

$$UCL_{\bar{x}} = \bar{\bar{X}} + A_2\bar{R}$$
$$= 73.7 + (0.58)(33.0)$$
$$= 73.7 + 19.14$$
$$= 92.84$$

$$LCL_x = \bar{\bar{X}} - A_2\bar{R}$$
$$= 73.7 - 19.14$$
$$= 54.56$$

$$UCL_R = D_4\bar{R}$$
$$= (2.11)(33.0)$$
$$= 69.63$$

$$LCL_R = D_3\bar{R}$$
$$= 0$$

Student Self-Monitoring of Daily Quiz Work

STEP 4

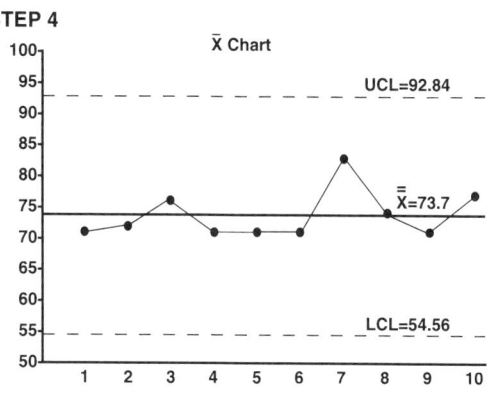

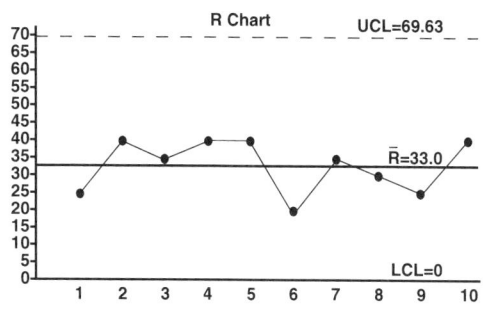

Construction/Interpretation Tips Control Chart

- Generally, collect 20-25 groups of samples before calculating the control limits.
- Upper and Lower Control Limits **MUST** be statistically calculated. Don't confuse them with specification limits, which are based on product or process requirements.
- Administration, through support and action, has the opportunity to control/reduce the natural variation between the control limits.
- Be sure to select the right type of Control Chart for the right type of data (see accompanying charts on pages 53-54).
- Data must be kept in the exact sequence as it was gathered, otherwise it is meaningless.
- Do not "tweak" the process beyond standard procedures while you are gathering the data; the data must reflect how it runs *naturally*.

TQM TEAMS, TOOLS, AND PROCESSES

Teams

In the pursuit of quality in the educational environment, school personnel will become involved with an essential component of the quality process: membership on a team. Teams provide the vehicle for using TQM to satisfy customer needs, involve all employees, and address the critical processes of the classroom, school, or district organization.

The effectiveness of teams is fundamental to the implementation of TQM in education. The adage that "two heads are better than one" speaks for the team process. All of us are always better than each of us. Teams study identified work processes in a structured environment that is designed to allow each team member to:

- contribute
- think creatively
- learn by collecting, sharing, and analyzing data
- develop the interpersonal skills so vital to effective teaming—listening, thinking, understanding, focusing, and creating solutions that work for their customers in schools

As teamwork grows, ideas are accepted, explored, expanded upon, piggybacked onto other ideas, and made more workable and productive.

The team enlarges the opportunity for a better solution through consensus—all members agree to support the decision of the team. This activity allows team members to take more control of their progress, and become more able to articulate the barriers that prevent them from doing their best work. Personal and team confidence grows as team members control processes, problems, and solutions, and see the results of their work in new process improvements being implemented. The team's contribution to the renewed health of its organization benefits the entire school-based community and moves the quality effort forward.

Characteristics for Successful Team Processing

- clearly established goals and objectives
- strong, effective, and efficient leadership
- creative blending of resources
- knowledge and application of quality tools
- statistical thinking
- disciplined documentation
- decision-making by consensus rather than by majority vote
- use of constructive criticism for feedback
- full and frank expression of ideas
- recognition of individuals for their contributions

The Team Process

The team process usually begins with the college/school's administrative steering committee creating an initial pilot project team. The chancellor or superintendent and his/her steering committee members generally choose several issues for teams to address. They also establish expectations, basic guidelines, and timetables for results. In addition, the administrative steering committee authorizes any resources the team will need. The issues that the steering committee chooses should be important to the team, and have the potential for a successful solution.

Using Tools in a Project Team

There are many data-based tools that can be used by teams as they address school issues for improvement. Those in *The Memory Jogger™ for Education* are the most frequently used for the purpose of gathering initial data on a process. The best time for a team to learn each of these tools is when the tool is needed, rather than being trained in them all at once. This just-in-time training allows each team member to maximize retention, fully participate, and contribute fresh ideas to the process.

The Plan-Do-Check-Act (PDCA) Cycle

The PDCA Cycle forms the basis for team efforts in problem solving. It represents the four steps necessary in addressing a desired system or process change.

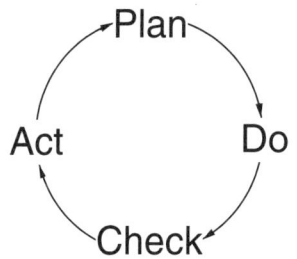

Plan-Do-Check-Act (PDCA) Cycle

1. **PLAN** - Plan a change aimed at an improvement in the school environment or process. What could be the most important accomplishment of the quality improvement team? What changes in an educational process might be desirable? What data can be gathered to study the change? Is new data needed? If yes, plan to record this new data, decide how you will use it, and in what process.

2. **DO** - Carry out the change or the test, preferably on a small scale. Search for data on hand that could answer the questions in Step 1.

3. **CHECK** - Check the results to see what was accomplished or learned. Observe or monitor the effects of the change.

4. **ACT** - Adopt the change, or abandon it if the results are not useful. Try the cycle again, with accumulated knowledge.

Basic Flow of Team Activity

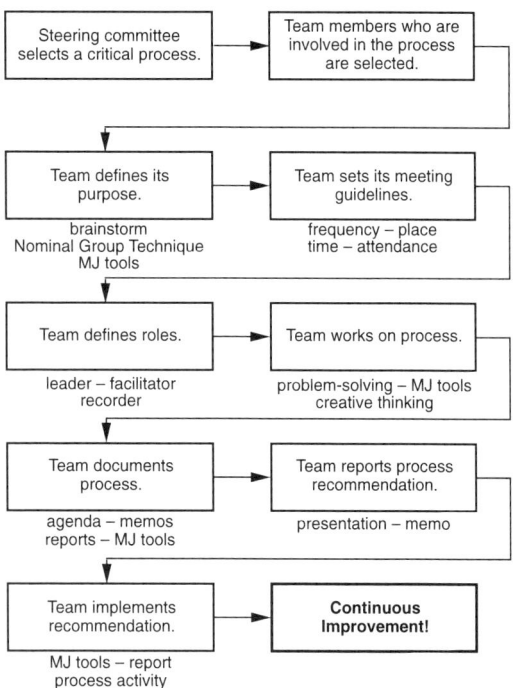

The following team presentation checklist identifies helpful hints for a presentation to administrators, colleagues, and others.

TEAM PRESENTATION CHECKLIST

— Invite key decision makers to the presentation.
  - By memo if appropriate
  - By phone the day before to confirm

— Arrange for the room.
  - Right size; large enough to be comfortable, not so large that group members are lost
  - Right atmosphere; the ideal is bright, quiet, clean, and informal

— Arrange for audiovisual (AV) equipment.
  - Flip chart
  - Overhead projector
  - Screen
  - Markers

— Prepare charts and AV materials.
  - Decide which charts will help the presentation
  - Assign responsibility
  - Keep AV materials simple in design

— Assign presentation responsibilities.

— Remember presentation guidelines.
  - Speak clearly and slowly
  - Listen to questions carefully; you will get an idea of what to stress in the presentation
  - Summarize new process recommendations simply and clearly

OTHER HELPFUL TOOLS
Brainstorming

All of the charting techniques we have described are thinking aids. They focus the attention of the user on the truly important dimensions of a problem. It is equally important, however, to expand your thinking to include **all** of the dimensions of a problem or solution. Brainstorming helps a group create many ideas in as short a time as possible.

Brainstorming can be used in two ways:
1. **Structured**—In this method, persons in a group must give an idea as their turn arises in the rotation or pass until the next round. It often forces even shy people to participate but can also create a certain amount of pressure to contribute.
2. **Unstructured**—In this method, group members simply give ideas as they come to mind. It tends to create a more relaxed atmosphere but also risks domination by the most vocal members.

In both methods the generally accepted guidelines are as follows:
- Never criticize ideas.
- Write every idea on a flip chart or blackboard. Having the words visible to everyone at the same time avoids misunderstandings and reminds others of new ideas.
- Everyone should agree on the question or issue being brainstormed. Write it down, too.
- Record on the flip chart in the words of the speaker; don't interpret.
- Do it quickly; 5-15 minutes works well.

Nominal Group Technique (NGT)

When selecting which problems to work on and in what order, the problem selected is often that of the person who speaks the loudest or who has the most authority. This might lead other team members to feel that *"their"* problem will never be worked on, which can lead to a lack of commitment to work on the problem selected, and the selection of the *"wrong"* problem in the first place. The **Nominal Group Technique** provides a way to give everyone in the group an equal voice in problem selection. The steps in the process are as follows:

1. Have everyone on the team write or say the problem that he/she feels is most important. If members of the team do not write the problems out, you need to record them on a flip chart or blackboard (or somewhere visible) as they are being communicated. If people do produce written problems, collect them when they are finished. Everyone may not feel comfortable writing, but anonymity may make them feel safer talking about sensitive problems.

2. Write the problem statements where the team can see them.

3. Check with the team to make sure that the same problem hasn't been written twice (it may have been written in slightly different words). If a problem is repeated, combine the two statements into one item.

4. Ask the team members to write on a piece of paper the letters corresponding to the number of problem statements the team produced. For example, if you ended up with five problem statements, everyone would write the letters "A" through "E" on the paper.

5. Make sure that each problem statement has a letter in front of it. Ask the team members to rank the problems

according to their importance, with "5" being most important, and "1" being least important. For example, the problem list may look like this:

    A. Space   D. Hiring
    B. Safety   E. Diversity
    C. Curriculum

Each member's paper would look like this:

    A. _____   D. _____
    B. _____   E. _____
    C. _____

If someone thought *"Hiring"* was the most important problem, he or she would write "5"; n the space for "D."

    A. _____   D. ____5_____
    B. _____   E. _____
    C. _____

Everyone then completes the list by voting what's second most important, third most important, etc. Each member's ranking is represented on the flip chart as shown:

    A. 2, 5, 2, 4, 1   D. 5, 2, 1, 1, 2
    B. 1, 4, 5, 5, 5   E. 3, 3, 4, 2, 3
    C. 4, 1, 3, 3, 4

An alternative ranking approach involves the "one half plus one" rule. Especially when dealing with many items, it may be necessary to limit the items to be considered. This rule suggests ranking only one half of the items plus one. For example, if 20 items were generated, team members would rank only 11 ideas.

6. Add up each line of numbers across. The item with the **highest** number is the most important one to the total team. In our example "B" (Safety) is the most important item with a total of 20. You should add up the numbers for each item and put them in order.

7. You would work on item B first, and then move through the list.

Force Field Analysis

How does change occur, either personally or organizationally? It's a dynamic process. It suggests movement, either from *"time A"* to *"time B"* or *"condition x"* to *"condition y."* Where does the energy for this "movement" come from? One approach is to view change as the result of a struggle between forces that are seeking to upset the status quo. This view is taken in the work of Kurt Lewin, who developed a technique called "Force Field Analysis." In it, Lewin proposed that "driving forces" move a situation toward change while "restraining forces" block that movement. When there is no change, the opposing forces are equal or the restraining forces are too strong to allow movement.

Consider the example of *"Why TQM for Education?"*:

Driving Forces	Restraining Forces
$$$$$ →	← Training for faculty
People are committed to doing their best →	← Parents' perceptions
	← Politics
Commitment to students →	← Tradition
	← Fear of change
Students have changed →	← Buy-in from top administration
Lack of structure →	← $$$$$
Reputation of TQM →	← Inability to agree on "who is our customer"
Pride in work →	
Competition →	← Staff's fear of additional responsibility
Less fear →	← Lack of time

If the restraining forces are stronger than the driving forces, then the desired change will not happen. It stands to reason that some change will occur if the driving forces are more powerful than the restraining forces.

Why does Force Field Analysis help make change happen?

1. It forces people to think together about all the facets of a desired change; it encourages creative thinking.
2. It encourages people to agree about the relative priority of restraining versus driving factors. The team can use the Nominal Group Technique to reach consensus quickly.
3. It provides a starting point for action.

How does Force Field Analysis accomplish this last task? One can approach change either from the perspective of strengthening "driving forces" or reducing the "restraining forces." Strengthening the positive often has the unexpected result of reinforcing the negative. Have you ever seen a situation where someone is told repeatedly that "X, Y, or Z" is bad for him or her? Instead of the desired improvement, it often strengthens resistance. Usually the most effective tactic is to diminish or eliminate a restraining force. In our example, it would be much more helpful to deal with *"lack of time"* than to constantly remind someone that *"students have changed."*

If done honestly, Force Field Analysis can be a helpful aid to thinking and a strategic tool for change.

PIE CHART

Pie Charts are simply graphs in which the entire circle represents 100% (not 360 degrees) of the data to be displayed. The circle (pie) is divided into percentage *slices* that clearly show the largest shares of data. This is useful in the same way as a Pareto Chart. Pie Charts are sometimes even more useful and are widely used to display data on TV or in the newspapers. As with all other graphs, be sure to clearly mark the subject matter, dates if needed, the percentages within the slices, and what each slice represents.

Pie Chart
Survey of Reaction to Class Registration Process

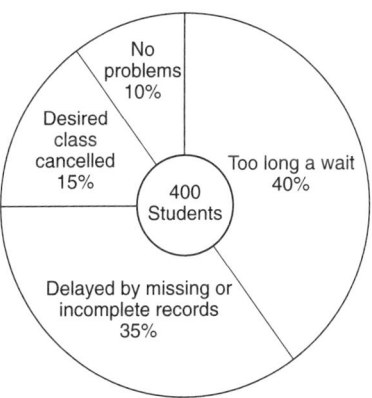

STRATIFICATION*

Stratification is often useful in analyzing data to find improvement opportunities. Stratification helps analyze cases in which data actually masks the real facts. This often happens when the recorded data is from many sources but is treated as one number.

For example, data on minor injuries at a school may be recorded as a single figure, but that number is actually the sum total of injuries:
- By type: cuts and burns
- By location: eyes, hands, feet, etc.
- By department: maintenance, athletics, science lab, etc.

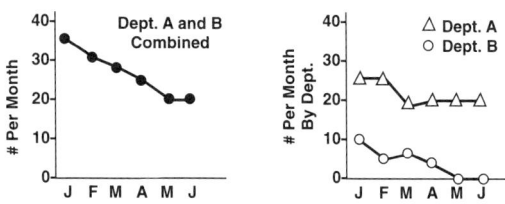

Stratification breaks down single numbers into meaningful categories or classifications to focus corrective action.

*See "Different Uses Of A Pareto Chart," pages 20-22, for stratification in Pareto analysis. Also see pages 172-174 of the AT&T *Statistical Quality Control Handbook* for examples of stratification in control chart patterns.

ADDITIONAL BAR GRAPHS
Compound Bar Graph

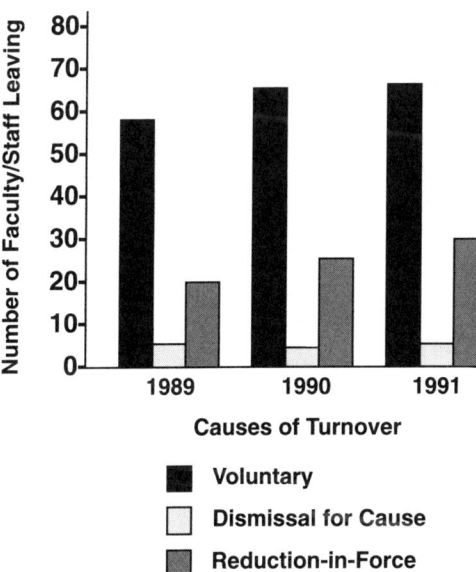

Horizontal Bar Graph

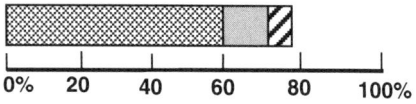

Salaries As A Percent Of Budget

Negative Numbers On A Bar Graph

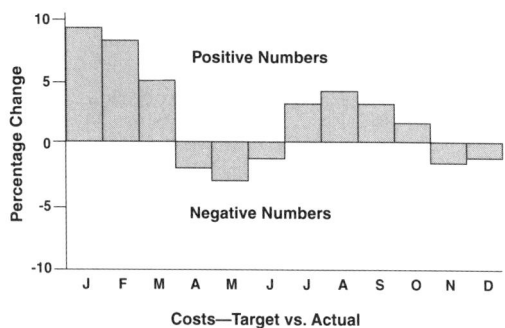

Construction/Interpretation Tips
Data Points to Ponder

- The aim of data-based problem solving is not to gather **more** data but to gather **meaningful** data.
- The collection and proper use of data short-circuits much of the interpersonal conflict that happens in groups.
- Data can be used to:
  — Understand the current **actual** situation (good and bad)
  — Regulate and modify the process
  — Accept or reject a product or process
- Bad data is worse than no data.
- Data should ideally be based on a truly random sample in which each event or piece has an equal chance of being observed or selected.
- Data that is compared must be gathered **consistently**.
- There are two major types of data, **measured/continuous** and **counted/discrete.**

Measured/ Continuous Data that's measured on a continuous scale such as length, weight, time, or scores.

Counted/ Discrete Data that is an accumulation of observations of a particular characteristic such as the number of errors, times late, typos, or missed calls.

- Every data collection document should include:
  — Name of person(s) collecting data
  — Date of collection
  — Time span covered, e.g., time of day
  — Location of data collection, e.g., department, office
  — Instruments (if applicable) or any other methods used

Construction/Interpretation Tips
Common Mistakes to Avoid

- Don't bias the results by the method of sampling. Try to gather sample data in as random a way as possible, e.g., don't take all the books from the top of the box.
- Don't confuse control limits with specification limits. Control limits are statistically determined whereas specification limits are based on what is needed or desired.
- Don't make it more complicated than it needs to be. Use the simplest appropriate tool.
- Don't collect too much or too little data. Don't collect data for a week when a day will do or vice versa.
- Don't overcomplicate graphs. Keep them simple and clear so that the message is apparent to the viewer.
- Don't confuse samples with populations.
- Don't blindly interpret graphs the same way in different situations. Use common sense, e.g., frequency of occurrence may not always be the most significant measure under the Pareto principle.
- Don't stand on a single statistic. Have other supporting evidence, e.g., find the range, not just the mean.
- Don't hesitate to seek help when a situation seems too complex or confusing for you to handle. Many institutions today have professional statisticians who can help you collect and analyze information in the most efficient and effective way possible.

GLOSSARY OF TERMS USED IN STATISTICAL PROCESS CONTROL

ATTRIBUTES are qualitative data that can be counted for recording and analysis. Examples include characteristics such as the presence of a required label and the distribution of required forms. Other examples include characteristics that are inherently measurable (i.e., could be treated as variables). Where the results are recorded in a simple yes/no fashion (such as class attendance), p, np, c, and u charts are used rather than an $\bar{X}$ and R chart (see Variables).

AVERAGE or mean is the most common expression of the centering of a distribution. It is signified by $\bar{X}$ and is calculated by totaling the observed values and dividing by the number of observations

$$\bar{X} = \frac{(X_1 + X_2 + \ldots + X_n)}{n}$$

BIMODAL DISTRIBUTION is one that has two identifiable curves within it, indicating a mixing of two populations such as different departments, teachers, or students.

*COMMON CAUSE is a source of variation that is always present; it is part of the random variation inherent in the process itself. Its origin can usually be traced to an element of the system that only administration can correct.

*CONTROL CHART is a graphic representation of a process characteristic, showing plotted values of some statistic gathered from that characteristic, and one or two control limits. It has two basic uses: as a judgment to determine if a process was in control, and as an aid in achieving and maintaining statistical control.

*CONTROL LIMIT is a line (or lines) on a control chart used as a basis for judging the significance of the variation from subgroup to subgroup. Variation beyond a control limit is evidence that special causes are affecting the process. Control limits are calculated from process data and are not to be confused with specifications or desired results.

*DETECTION or INSPECTION is a past-oriented strategy that attempts to identify unacceptable output after it has been produced and separate it from the good output, such as test scores/grades (see also PREVENTION).

DISTRIBUTION is the population (universe) from which observations are drawn, categorized into cells, and form identifiable patterns. It is based on the concept of variation that states that anything measured repeatedly will arrive at different results. These results will fall into statistically predictable patterns. A *bell-shaped curve* (normal distribution) is an example of a distribution in which the greatest number of observations fall in the center with fewer and fewer observations falling evenly on either side of the average.

FORCE FIELD ANALYSIS is a technique developed by Kurt Lewin that displays the driving (positive) and restraining (negative) forces surrounding any change. This is displayed in a "balance sheet" format.

FREQUENCY DISTRIBUTION is a statistical table that presents a large volume of data in such a way that the central tendency (average/mean/median) and distribution are clearly displayed.

NOMINAL GROUP TECHNIQUE is a weighted ranking technique that allows a team to prioritize a large number of issues without creating "winners" and "losers."

NONCONFORMITIES, sometimes called discrepancies or faults, are specific occurrences of a condition that does not conform to specifications or other inspection standards. An individual nonconforming unit can have the potential for more than one nonconformity (e.g., a report could have several typos, a cafeteria could have any number of furniture problems). The c and u charts are used to analyze systems producing nonconformities.

POPULATION is the universe of data under investigation from which a sample will be taken.

PREVENTION is a future-oriented strategy that improves quality by directing analysis and action toward correcting the process. Prevention is consistent with a philosophy of never-ending improvement (see DETECTION).

PROCESS is the combination of faculty, staff, administration, students, instruction, curriculum, methods, and environment that produces a given product or service.

RANGE is a measure of the variation in a set of data. It is calculated by subtracting the lowest value in the data set from the highest value in that same set.

RUNS are the patterns in a Run Chart or Control Chart within which a number of points line up on only one side of the central line. Beyond a certain number of statistically-based consecutive points the pattern becomes unnatural and worthy of attention.

*SAMPLE is one or more individual events or measurements selected from the output of a process for purposes of identifying characteristics and performance of the whole.

*SIGMA $\hat{\sigma}$ is the Greek letter used to designate the estimated standard deviation.

*SPECIAL CAUSE, also known as an assignable cause, is a source of variation that is intermittent, unpredictable, unstable. It is signalled by a point beyond the control limits.

SPECIFICATION is the requirement for judging acceptability of a particular characteristic. Chosen with respect to functional or customer requirements for the product/service, a specification may or may not be consistent with the demonstrated capability of the process (if it is not, out-of-specification products/services are certain to result). A specification should never be confused with a control limit.

*STANDARD DEVIATION is a measure of the spread of the process output or the spread of a sampling statistic from the process (e.g., of subgroup averages), denoted by the Greek letter $\hat{\sigma}$ (sigma) for the estimated standard deviation.

*STATISTICAL CONTROL is the condition a process is in when all special causes have been removed, evidenced on a control chart by the absence of points beyond the control limits and by the absence of non-random patterns or trends within the control limits.

*STATISTICAL PROCESS CONTROL is the use of statistical techniques, such as Control Charts, to analyze a process or its output so as to take appropriate actions to achieve and maintain a state of statistical control and to improve the capability of the process.

STRATIFICATION is the process of classifying data into subgroups based on characteristics or categories.

TRENDS are the patterns in a Run Chart or Control Chart that feature the continued rise or fall of a series of points. Like Runs, attention should be paid to such patterns when they exceed a statistically-based predetermined number.

VARIABLES are those characteristics of a product or service that can be measured. Examples are scores, behavior, time, and length (see also ATTRIBUTES).

***VARIATION** is the inevitable difference among individual outputs of a process. The sources of variation can be grouped into two major classes: common causes and special causes.

*From Ford Motor Company's *Q101* (1983). This is a handbook of quality requirements for Ford's manufacturing plants and outside vendors.

Customization of Your GOAL/QPC Books

Customize GOAL/QPC products with your company's name and logo, mission or vision statement, and almost anything else.

Benefits of customization
- Allows you more flexibility in determining content
- Gives your leaders an opportunity to personalize every copy
- Helps to promote your company's quality improvement efforts
- Communicates your organization's commitment to quality
- Helps lower the costs of in-house development of training materials
- Helps employees understand how they can help achieve company goals
- Gives teams a common vision

A few details
- Please allow a minimum of *4 weeks* for delivery of customized products.
- Customization is most cost effective for quantities of *200 or more.*
- Ask us about customizing GOAL/QPC products in other languages.

Call Toll Free: 800-643-4316
Phone: 603-893-1944 or Fax: 603-870-9122
E-mail: service@goalqpc.com
Web site: www.goalqpc.com

The Memory Jogger™ II

This pocket guide is designed to help you improve the procedures, systems, quality, cost, and yields related to your job. *The Memory Jogger™ II* combines the basic Quality Tools and the Seven Management and Planning Tools in an easy-to-use format. It includes continuous improvement tools such as Cause and Effect, Histogram, Run Chart, Pareto Chart, and many more!

Code: 1030E

The Team Memory Jogger™

Easy to read and written from the team member's point of view, *The Team Memory Jogger™* goes beyond basic theories to provide you with practical nuts-and-bolts action steps on preparing to be an effective team member, how to get a good start, get work done in teams, and when and how to end a project. *The Team Memory Jogger™* also teaches you how to deal with problems that can arise within a team. It's perfect for all employees at all levels.

Code: 1050E

Quantity discounts are available.

Improving the Way Organizations Run

GOAL/QPC is a leading, worldwide provider of information, tools, and services for organizational improvement. We are a not-for-profit research, publishing, and training company dedicated to helping people achieve performance excellence.

Our best-selling product line, The Memory Jogger™ series, is designed to give everyone in the organization the tools and methods for organizational improvement. We also provide off-the-shelf training materials, software, books, videotapes, and training courses to help you meet your improvement goals.

Visit our web site today and learn how people around the world, in all types of organizations and industries, use our materials for:
- Process Management and Improvement
- Problem Solving
- Project Management
- ISO 9001:2000 Compliance
- Strategic Planning
- Team Facilitation and Coaching
- Customer Focus
- Innovation and Creativity
- Six Sigma
- Lean Enterprise

Toll Free: 800-643-4316
Sales Direct: 603-893-1944 • Fax: 603-870-9122
service@goalqpc.com • www.goalqpc.com